*• The Wizard
Magic Channe
with the T*

ALSO BY JASON D MCKEAN

Audio Albums and Meditations

OM Sanctuary
OM Eternity
108 Sacred OMs
OM Serenity
OMdigenous
OM Cosmos
OM Beats
OM Shiva Shakti Namaha

New Day Meditation Series
OM Resonance Meditation Series

---

www.JasonDMcKean.com

THE WIZARD'S HANDBOOK

Magic Channel Tarot Reading with the Tarot Wizard

JASON D McKEAN

McK

Copyright © 2021
By Jason D McKean
1st Printing by McKean Productions LLC, June 2021

Library of Congress Control Number: 2021909346

All rights reserved. No part of the book may be reproduced or transmitted in any form or by any means, electronic or mechanical, including photocopying, recording, digitally, or by any information storage and retrieval system, without permission in writing from the Publisher.

Jason D McKean
Box 71
Malibu CA 90265

Cover photo: Robert Yager
Illustrations: Jason D McKean

ISBN: 9798746472885
Printed by KDP / Amazon

DEDICATION

*To my beloved wife Sumire, thank you
for making all things possible.*

*To my loving Parents, thank you
for bringing me into creation
and giving me space to create.*

*To my blessed Family, thank you
for bringing joy and great adventures.*

*To my dear Friends, thank you
for your deep wisdom mixed with fun times.*

*To all my Teachers, Students, and Querents,
thank you! I learn from all of you.
We are all on this journey together!*

Table of Contents

Introduction 9
Why Read Tarot? 13
What's At Your Core? 14
Tarot Is An Exploration 15
The Three Basic Steps 16
Tarot Is Serious Fun! 18
Keep It Simple 19
The Cards Have Their Say Too 20
Major Arcana 22
Archetypes 23
Minor Arcana 24
The Suits 25
The Wands 26
The Cups 27
The Swords 28
The Pentacles 29
The Elements 30
The Three Card Spread 32
It's All In The Question 35
Patterns 36
Opening Your Intuition 37
Three Cards At The Top 38
Who Gets To Touch The Cards? 40
Past, Present, and Future 42
Creating Ritual 43
The Flow of Energy 44

- Building Consciousness 46
- Cultivating Your Relationship with Spirit 48
- The Ability To Channel 50
- Fate or Free Will 52
- "That Which Works" 53
- Everyone Is A Work In Progress 55
- The Spectrum of Human Experience 58
- The Spirit of Co-Creation 61
- Success! 62
- Reading Reversals 63
- Letting Go Is Essential 66
- Human Beings Are A Verb 69
- Making Friends With The Unknown 71
- Commit To The Meaning 73
- Give What You Get 74
- Uh Oh, I Just Drew One of THOSE Cards 76
- Career or Job? 78
- The Reflecting Pool 81
- Common Threads That Run Through the Cards..... 83
- The Vault 84
- Keep Yourself Out Of The Reading 86
- Who Wants A History Lesson? 88
- No One Is A Statue In Stone 91
- Opening Up To New Card Meanings 92
- Permission Granted 95
- Magical Answers? 97
- Words Specific To Tarot 99
- Bio 100

Introduction

If you have picked up this book and want to find out the history of Tarot, and look for card meanings and new spreads, well … this is not that book.

If you are looking to know why the Tarot cards have called you, then I hope to be able to shed some light in that area.

Why am I the Tarot Wizard? Because I choose to be and because it has chosen me. I can live with both paths inside me. One path fulfills an individual ambition of having a creative life and the other fulfills a call to be of service. Both paths intersect at a deep desire to understand the mysteries of life, not to intellectually dismantle them, but rather to embrace them and find one's best self in them.

My personal calling as the Tarot reader has been one of many twists and turns. Most of the discoveries in this book took place inside of me, when I had no idea where I was headed. Along the way, the path revealed itself to me, much like the journey of the Fool.

I'm not the heavy-handed rules and regulations type of reader. There are established practices and rituals for card cleansing, and preparation before reading, and other do's and don'ts that have been part of the practices of the Tarot for many years. But having read for thousands of people, my process has been one of trial and error and finding what worked for me. I only got into trouble if I copied techniques of other readers, so I looked to find my own voice and my own way of doing things.

Finding out who you are as a reader and why you read Tarot is what it's all about. So read on and I hope that you find inspiration and light.

The illustrations in this book are from my own hand. Some of them are the accepted alchemical symbols, others I created for my own purposes. I encourage you to invent ways to keep the knowledge straight within your own being.

Jason D McKean
Malibu, CA 2021

(PS: You can read this book from cover to cover, or turn to any page as a meditation or an oracle and see where Spirit is leading you ...)

"Create Sacred Space"

Why Read Tarot?

It's good for you to know why you want to read Tarot. Are you naturally that go-to person with your friends, the adviser, the one that everyone brings their problems to? Are you the person that strangers will come up to and ask questions? Are you naturally curious about human motivation, and why we do what we do?

If you have a natural inclination to be with others, to take them seriously, and deal with problems or difficult situations they may find themselves in, then these are good foundations for doing the work of reading Tarot.

If you don't care for people, or find the situations they're in as bothersome or boring, then being a Tarot reader will not be a great fit. This is the essence of it. Most people do not come to a Tarot reader if their life is going great. They will come to get answers regarding a serious issue or to know if they are on the right path. On occasion, you'll get asked to put a spell on someone, or provide the lucky lotto winning numbers (that's on you if you provide those services). I read Tarot because it gives me a platform to have transformative and healing discussions with others. And because I enjoy it.

What's At Your Core?

What motivates you? Do you like helping people? Are you a good listener? Is it fun to sit with others and talk about their lives? Are you able to know details about someone without them telling you? Does the Tarot speak to you in ways that other symbol systems do not?

It can all be true even if sometimes we don't know all of the reasons. But that can be part of the journey, part of why we do anything. So that we can discover deeper parts of our self, and see what's truly at our core. And reading the Tarot will give you insight into your own life, as much as it offers insight for others.

Hear what you're saying to others. The messages that you create, the advice you give, this is all stemming from you. You and your relationship with your spiritual source.

What does that relationship look like? Is it healthy, nurturing, expansive? Is it combative, uncertain, limiting? Some of it may look easy, other parts of it complex. Working on your relationship with your spiritual source is an essential ingredient to reading the Tarot. And not coincidentally, to living a long, sustained and fulfilled life.

Tarot Is An Exploration

Reading Tarot is an act of creation, and one of creating sacred space for another, so as to see their life reflected back to them through evocative images and solid archetypes.

The reader sets the stage and let's unfold a message in the moment. The reader is a guide, the reader is a mirror. Inviting a querent to see their path forward with fresh eyes so they can see the part they play in their life. So they can value what it is they're feeling about in their life. And from the seeing and feeling, that action can be taken to connect fully with their life.

The Three Basic Steps

Even though I don't consider myself to be a stickler for the rules, I believe there are **three basics steps** to follow. And I think these are important and can be used as a guide to be able to sustain a long and healthy relationship with the Tarot.

The first step is that we see each other as spiritual beings.

The second step is that we are not to condemn another person to a specific pattern of behavior for all time.

And the third step is to let go of creating a specific outcome. The cards will have their say, so let them speak.

There can be a temptation to want to bring people to a level that we see as fitting for them, based on our own journey and on a timetable that we're looking to impose. But not everyone operates at the same frequency or speed that we do. As a reader, it's okay to be aware of this within yourself because it shows what you value, but it's not up to you to judge another's progress. Not everyone is at the same place on the spiritual path.

"One does not 'use' the Tarot as a tool.

One builds a relationship with it."

Tarot Is Serious Fun!

Tarot is fun! It's a blast to be able to read the cards for others and seek wisdom. But are there certain responsibilities to it?

Yes, absolutely.

I've had clients come to me and say that they remember their reading from 20 years before by another psychic. 20 years! Most of us will have a difficult time remembering what we had for breakfast, much less 20 years ago.

People remember their readings. So take it seriously, and take responsibility for the words that you say.

Keep It Simple

Just because something is simple, does not lessen its effect or make it any less powerful. The way forward has a lot of choices involved. In order to successfully navigate these choices, one can move forward in a step by step manner. You as a reader might see the outcome. But the querent needs to see their part in the actions they take to bring about the outcome.

Use language that is understandable, universal, and gets to the underlying issue. This will be of great help to your querent. I've had sessions from readers before who spoke in metaphysical flourishes that sounded pretty, but I didn't know what the heck they were saying.

A large part of any counseling is to match a frequency (a vibe) of the other person, so that what you say can be heard and understood. It's like tuning into a radio station on an old-time transistor radio. And you mustn't think of it as being manipulative, it's about picking up on the heart of the matter and where someone is coming from. It's what a natural empath will do anyway, to tune into the energy of another, and speak on a level that is getting through. It's just working with your natural gifts in a capacity to be of service for others.

THE CARDS HAVE THEIR SAY TOO

I'm not going to lie. There are times when I'd love for specific cards to show up in the exact position I'd like them to. But I should know better.

The blind process of the Tarot is such that the cards can have their say, and not be directed by our ego. If we were to direct a reading from our own need for everything to fit, then we would perhaps lose information that is helpful to the querent. I've had those readings where I've pulled a card and thought "I wouldn't have pulled this, is this a mistake?" I've then gone on to talk about it, and find out that it makes perfect sense to the querent.

Who are we reading for? Our self or for them? It only has to make sense for the querent in how they can work through their own situation. You don't read Tarot because it's comfortable and easy, that is for sure. You read it to help bring light to areas of uncertainty.

Certain cards will surface because they need to be seen and tell their story. So do your part and give voice to that story without judgement and with a pure desire to let that card's energy be of service to your querent.

"Connection is Key"

Major Arcana

The 22 cards of the Major Arcana represent the Fool's Adventure, the Hero's Journey, the Cycle of Experience. One starts off on the adventure without knowing the outcome, just heading out on a wing and a prayer. They're called towards a direction, listening and moving accordingly. As they go deeper onto the trail, they meet a cast of differing personalities and circumstances that help them to clarify what they've been searching for all along. Traveling through hardship and triumph, insight and wisdom, the trail ends with the successful reaching of the goal, and then begins again with the next quest.

The Fool represents the part of us that is unknowing of how all the details will work out as we follow our own soul's calling. We have our goals and will have to run the gauntlet in order to achieve them. There will be help along the way for the times we need it, but we will also have to take ownership of our personal power to move through the difficult times to overcome them.

The cycles never end, the wheel always turns. There is always a new horizon to look out onto, and new territory to rise into. The Soul's Journey is an eternal progression.

ARCHETYPES

The Major Arcana is filled with personality types or Archetypes. Archetypes represent singular attributes of a personality, ones like the Emperor or the Empress or the Hermit, along with the cards that espouse a certain value, such as Justice or Temperance or Strength.

These cards are often seen as strong indicators of what the querent is having to build up in themselves to move through their situation.

As one gains clarity in their goals, a personality can be worn and activated in any situation to help you navigate through it. If you need to be more assertive, you'll ride the Chariot. If you're needing to be more introspective, you'll wear the cloak of the Hermit. If your world starts to crumble and fall, you'll need the resolve of the Tower to pick up and rebuild.

Because we are always in motion as energetic beings, there is the freedom to be any or all of the multitude of personalities in order to get done what needs to get done. We may have one or two strong connections to a main archetype, but there is room to draw in what's needed. Movement through this Cycle of the Tarot lends itself to strong character development.

Minor Arcana

The Minor Arcana is made up of the Four Suits of the Tarot; the Wands, the Cups, the Swords, and the Pentacles.

The Soul, the Emotions, the Mind, and the Body.

Four suits, each starting with an Ace and moving up through a cycle to the Ten card. Each suit has an additional group of Royalty or Court cards, with a Page, Knight, Queen and King. It is my preference to set the Royalty cards aside from the main cycle of each suit, since they have a lot more going on with them.

The cycle of the suits in the Minor Arcana allows you to see what energies are most active in a situation, and what intelligence center is at play within a querent. Are they in a mental space, or emotional state, is this helping them or holding them back with what they're wrestling with?

You can get a full picture of the progress of fulfillment just by studying the Minor Arcana. Look to see how we can integrate all of the parts of self into one healthy human experience.

And why does everyone fear the Swords? Don't hate on the Swords please.

The Suits

The Wands = the Soul

The Cups = the Heart Center

The Swords = the Mind

The Pentacles = the Body

The Wands

The Suit of the Wands gets to our very core, showing us where our spark is and where our passions lie. It is the fuel that inspires us to wake up every day and feed the vision of our place in the world. It is the light that reveals the path for us on how to take action in that world.

Areas covered by the Wands:

- Soul
- Creativity
- Career
- Purpose
- Motivation
- Passion

THE CUPS

The Suit of the Cups shows us how to invest the best parts of ourselves into the relationships that will be significant and life-changing. It is how we connect, on the deepest levels, to heal and help each other. It is how we show up in our most authentic self to give and receive love.

Areas covered by the Cups:

- Heart
- Emotions
- Spirituality
- Connection
- Love
- Healing

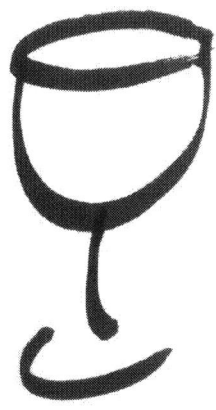

The Swords

The Suit of the Swords looks to be such a dicey suit, with so many negative images. The Mind is a complex part of our being, mainly because it wants to plan out our future, and be in control of how events will unfold. It's the planner part of us (just hope everything goes as planned).

Areas covered by the Swords:

- Mind
- Identity
- Intellect
- Perception
- Communication
- Mindset

THE PENTACLES

The Suit of the Pentacles is where the rubber meets the road, and we look to see how our inner self comes out to play. Solidifying ideals, manifesting desires and being able to sustain our lives. The Pentacles is how we know we're making progress in life, and reaching our goals.

Areas covered by the Pentacles:

- Body
- Physical
- Manifestation

- Wealth
- Outside World
- Actions

The Elements

The Four Suits of the Tarot are associated with the Four Elements:

Wands = **Fire** *(Soul)*

Cups = **Water** *(Heart)*

Swords = **Air** *(Mind)*

Pentacles = **Earth** *(Body)*

"Your words affect others"

The Three Card Spread

Not to sound harsh, but this Tarot Wizard doesn't care for the Celtic Cross. For me, it's too time consuming and locks the cards within a structure that is too limiting. With the three card spread, one has more flexibility in how to interact with the Tarot.

The number 3 is very powerful because of our associations with storytelling. All stories have a beginning, middle and end. The Tarot cards are natural story tellers, with each image giving a direct message or a mysterious clue as to the quality of passage on one's journey. And all querents like to see how their story will end up!

Three cards are a perfect amount of information, just enough for clarity with no clutter.

*"Give
&
Take
is present in
every relationship"*

*"Look for that
which is Healing,
Helpful and Hopeful."*

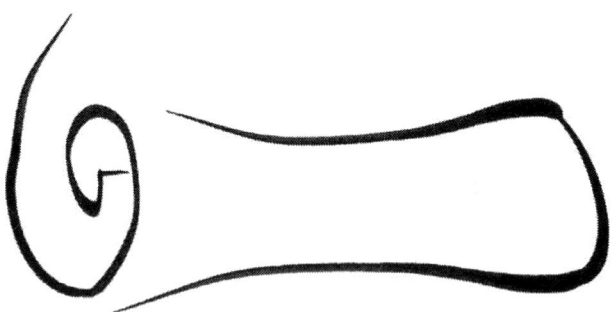

It's All In The Question

To find relevant answers, one must know the question. And asking a GOOD question is imperative with the Tarot!

Here is an example of a terrible question to ask: *"Will I ever find love?"*

Why is this such a terrible question? For one, the soul is eternal and eternity is such a very long time. So of course one will find love at some point. Finding and keeping love are different situations though.

Here are some examples of a much better way of asking this question ...

"Am I taking the steps to be a better relationship partner?"

"What can help me build my confidence in myself?"

"Am I able to express my feelings in a clear manner to my partner or prospective partners?"

See the difference? And it works for all areas of life too.

PATTERNS

Let a story unfold because you see a pattern before you. Whether you pull two cards, three cards, five cards, look to see where the patterns are emerging. Depending upon our language, we're trained to read text in a certain direction. But reading Tarot can be a different animal.

One can open themselves up to seeing patterns and layers of intensity. Sometimes one card is predominant and supported by the surrounding cards. If a card stands out as a starting point, then build a message on that one. Begin at the beginning and talk about this card that you're connecting with. Move on from there.

If reading a 3-card spread, there may be two Royalty cards bookending a Minor arcana card. Or two Minor arcanas with a Major arcana in the center. Things get exciting when two negative looking cards are surrounding a positive card. Open yourself up to seeing how the energies oppose or complement each other.

The reader makes the call.

There's no right way to look at the patterns. There's only you trusting how to craft your message.

Opening Your Intuition

Our intuition can take many forms. Sometimes we'll have a mini-vision in our mind's eye, and sometimes we'll hear words being whispered into our ear. Other times we have a sense of knowing that we'll give voice to. How is it that you best connect to your intuition?

It's important to have a clarity of being, feeling well and healthy and being unattached to negative emotion. Taking care of your bodily temple assures that your spiritual connection will be strong, and have the power to transmit across the vast expanse of space and time.

Three Cards At The Top

With every reading that I do, I like to take a look at the energy of the querent. Even if the querent is asking about another person. (Sometimes especially if the querent is asking about another person.) I like to see where they're coming from. So three cards will be pulled at the onset.

Those initial three cards have a world of information in them. You can glean info about what's at a querent's core, or what brings them to your table, the situation that they are moving through. And keep those first three cards in mind during the rest of the reading. You might refer back to what it is they're going through and how they can respond. It's not that they're necessarily outcome cards, but it can show what they have in their personality to work with, while engaged in their situation.

TIPS & TRICKS

*To expand your personal
knowledge of the Tarot,
read on Concepts.*

*Pull cards on ideas like
Compassion,
Freedom,
Suffering.*

*See what cards come up.
Dig deep and
let new layers of
understanding flow in.*

Who Gets To Touch The Cards?

How do we pick the cards, and do we let the querent touch them? Some readers don't like to have their cards touched by anyone else but them. And that's fine. When I'm doing a live reading, I'm all about letting querents choose cards for themselves. Not all the cards, but I am open in how I direct a session. I'll let my intuition guide me as to which cards I pick, and which ones they pick.

I think that it gives the querent a sense of involvement, that they're a participant in their own life. That events are not just happening to them, there are choices they can make within those events. Choosing cards gives them a say in how they can move forward.

If you have an established setting for your readings, you can have a few decks around, and decide which ones can be open to the touch of your querents, and which ones are only to be touched by you. If you feel a special connection to a deck, that only you work with, so be it. Some decks will tell you that they want to be treated in a certain manner, so be open to this communication and let them be heard. Again, the Tarot is not a tool, it is a partnership in opening up paths of spiritual awareness.

*"If you think you can't,
then you can't.*

*If you know you can,
then you can."*

Past, Present, and Future

*"Our past becomes our future,
unless we change it in the present"*

It can be tempting to read the Tarot in a way of categorizing the past, the present, the future, as if they are separate parts of a person's life. But if a person is stuck in certain behaviors, they're just going to repeat them over and over. One doesn't just change because of the passing of time. They change because they recognize that it's time to break old habits, release outdated thoughts, and begin a daily process of altering the patterns.

The present is where the heavy lifting is done.

Empowering the present is the guideline for creating a brighter future. We don't have to be prisoners to our past. The Tarot helps to pinpoint the parts of self that we can focus on bettering in the present. We may see a need to get inspired, or follow a stricter plan, or find a personal space. To be in a flow of energy, we build up our inner fire to fuel our vision, and activate a part of it day by day. One thing leads to another, and the magical leap to a better future happens because we take the time to care in the present about our progress.

CREATING RITUAL

I have said before that I'm not a regulations and rules Wizard, but I think that having meaningful rituals as part of your Tarot routine will serve you well as you're creating Sacred Space.

Here are some of mine, and I welcome you to see the value for yourself or not.

Having an opening intention or prayer is a beautiful way to start a reading. It lets your querent know you're looking out for their well-being and that you care about their progress. My opening intention is "We ask that the Tarot cards speak to your highest good." This is said after I have created a connection by activating the Chi around us (Chi or Qi is spiritual energy).

I will place talismans and crystals on my table as a touchstone of my experience and my calling. They are mostly Skeleton Keys that I've collected over the years, but there are other items that hold significance to my role as a Tarot reader. I will connect with them for info if called to.

I will close a reading with a tight summation of the main aspects of the reading, and say "I hope this has been of service to you," and then offer them a chance to photograph their card spread.

THE FLOW OF ENERGY

All life is energy. When there's a consistent flow of energy, our life runs smoothly. When we have a goal that we're working towards and our spirit is aligned with that goal, then there is an open channel. When our mental state is in agreement with the goals we're moving toward, the path is an open channel of our energy.

When our physical body is strong and up to the task, that too is an open channel. When our heart space is open and we're connecting with the right people, our energy is open and flowing in a forward direction. If any of these areas are partly blocked or closed down, then that is where problems occur.

Because the Tarot represents the wide spectrum of human activity, we can look to see where a consistent flow of energy can be open or blocked. We can see if our motivation is high or if it's flagging within the suit of the Wands. The Swords can inform us if we're getting in our own way by overthinking our moves with too many plans. The Cups let us know how our emotional state is lifting us up or dragging us down. And we can see if our hopes and plans are making it out into the world as an act of manifestation, with the help of the Pentacles.

*Look to see
the Energy
behind the Words,
the Framework
behind the Facade,
the True Character
behind the Mask.*

BUILDING CONSCIOUSNESS

What is consciousness? Simply put, it is an ability to witness ourselves in action. One can think of it as the layer of Self that has an overview of our mechanical being. We aren't normally conscious of our heart beating, or of our breathing, or how our brain thinks it's thoughts. But we can be conscious of those thoughts, and if those thoughts are to our benefit or if they hold us back in life.

How can we see a clear example of this? I often use the analogy of driving a car on the Freeway. We're driving along, minding our own business, when suddenly, a car pulls RIGHT IN FRONT, and we have to slam on our brakes! Think of how angry we get in that moment. If we had the power to manifest some bad things with our thoughts ... well ... watch out! You sit there in anger and curse and fantasize horrible thoughts, and then rant about it all day with everyone. But what if you catch your self getting mad, and say "Wow, that was uncool. But I've driven like that before. I'm going to let it go." And then let it go.

Think of when you say something that "triggers" your partner who automatically gets upset. What triggers you? Are you able to take a step back and see what's happening on a deeper level?

*"You are
the Key
AND
the Lock.*

*You have
the Answer
to all
of your
Questions"*

CULTIVATING YOUR RELATIONSHIP WITH SPIRIT

When reading Tarot, it's important to develop a relationship with Spirit or a spiritual source. This is in recognition that we don't do the work alone. Opening yourself up to a spiritual source is a way of developing trust. And it's in this trust that we start to deepen our connection to others.

If one doesn't know where to begin, doing a meditation for finding your spiritual source is a good way to start this connection.

Let's say you don't have a spiritual source, one you recognize anyway. In meditation, you can open up to a virtue that you look highly upon. A virtue such as patience, hard work, kindness, or honesty. Take a look at what these mean to you, how they make you feel, how you can activate them while reading Tarot.

You don't have to associate a personality with these ideals, such as having a Spirit Guide or Spiritual Master that personifies them. It's only important to know that you're connected to a higher source of positivity and you're working to include that vibration in your messages.

*"Our Heart Center
is where we
Connect with others,
activate our Compassion,
look to Heal one another,
and join together in Spirit.*

*Reading Tarot is as
Heart Center as it gets."*

The Ability to Channel

If one of your abilities is to be able to channel, then by all means, bring it in and allow it to complement your work with the Tarot.

What is it to channel? One is basically a conduit, an open pipeline to voice the unique wisdom of a Spiritual Master, or a Galactic Entity. It's not to be confused necessarily with mediumship, which is speaking with the dearly departed.

Many a time I've channeled messages that I had no recollection of afterwards. And whether you are conscious or channeling a message, both can be valid. It's always about the resonance and the integrity of the message anyway, it shouldn't matter where it's coming from.

Tips & Tricks

*Look at the
flow of energy
in the cards.*

*Is the path clear,
or are there obstacles?*

*Can one move freely,
or do they need to hold up
and check their surroundings?*

FATE OR FREE WILL

Is the future written and set in stone? Or do we have the ability to write our own destiny? The Tarot indicates frameworks, cycles, a structure in patterns that are repeated over and over. Are we locked into certain cycles and trapped within our programming? Are we free to move about these frameworks, choosing our movement in the moment? Or was it all pre-programmed from the very beginning?

Can it be both? Our physical DNA is encoded within to unfold over time, but our actions can alter that. Our immediate environment or diet can influence how our body develops.

We may be destined to meet a significant person at a certain point, but how that relationship unfolds is dependent on the people involved. Our soul can be mapped out with many potential meeting points for people and events, but there can be a part of us that chooses "yes" or "no" to activating it when the time comes.

The Tarot has a way of tapping into that soul map, and divining the potentials before you're aware of them. It doesn't mean that you're going to take the opportunity when it shows up. It just means to prepare yourself to say "yes."

"That Which Works"

People will ask me what the best way to do something is. I tell them that I am a big fan of "that which works."

And in Tarot, I can apply it to spreads, shuffling, the process of choosing cards, letting your querent touch your cards, if it's being recorded, if they can take a photo of the cards, and all other rituals and procedures of giving a reading.

There's also the question of if you should buy yourself a deck, or have it gifted to you. What if you're out in a store and don't have any one to buy it for you?

And how do you clear the energy of a reading off your cards, to prepare for the next one? Do you burn Sage or Palo Santo, or store your cards on Selenite?

Even though students can get overwhelmed with the proper etiquette of Tarot, I believe in leaving it up to them, and trust that they'll find their own areas to pay attention to, and not get too stuck on the "rules."

I've learned what works for me mostly by doing. The same will be true for you.

*"Honor your past.
It brought you this far."*

EVERYONE IS A WORK IN PROGRESS

When we listen to others speak, we can hear their hopes and fears. No one of us is perfect, none of us have it ALL together.

As a reader of Tarot, we have in our hands the opportunity to help our querent realize their potential. Our words have the power to help someone or hold them back from their goals. It's quite natural for one to get close to a goal, and then freeze up. I feel that's a common time for a querent hoping to be on the right path.

Sometimes we see their road ahead as difficult, with many challenges. How we speak of these harder times can help them set the stage for clarity inside themselves, or help them take action towards their goal. It can feel like one is a coach giving a pep talk during the big game, or encouraging a first-timer to take the plunge off the high-dive. Patience is key. Not everyone is ready to jump at the onset.

It is up to them to see the final version of who they're becoming, or the completed task that they're moving towards. It is not on us to judge the worthiness of their goal, only to see that they're aligned with it in confidence and clarity.

Appreciate the level that you are at.

Through experience, you'll grow to the next level.

Tips & Tricks

The Pages are Messengers.
See them as an opportunity to open
up to others with our authentic self.

Our voice becomes
a Sacred Vibration
that signals the Universe
who we are and what
we're looking to accomplish.

When we're aligned within,
what we say has the ability
to create our path before us.

Are you connecting
to your own Voice?

The Spectrum of Human Experience

The Tarot represents a full spectrum of human experience, from joy to suffering, from our highs to our lows, when we need to take action and when we need moments of reflection. The Tarot has it all, showing the moments when we are standing in our glory and when we're having dark nights of the soul. Every card has a purpose, every card has a message.

I do not fear pulling any of the "heavy cards", nor do I wish for only the "light cards" to make their appearance. The space that is created for understanding a querent's situation is open for a full examination of all the energies at play. To help someone move through any difficulty, the Tarot reader takes that information and weaves a meaningful message with it.

Imagine playing only certain notes on a piano to keep it in a certain range of emotion. Wouldn't you feel cheated? Imagine going to a Tarot reader and they tell you only good things are going to happen. Would that feel authentic? Read the full range of life's experiences, and give your querent the ability to see how all the energies will play a part in creating their future, with all the available information to work with.

*"Not everyone is
at the same place
on the
spiritual path."*

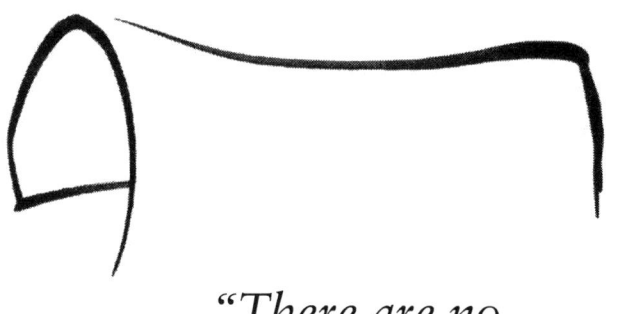

*"There are no
coincidences
in Life.
So it is with
the Tarot."*

The Spirit of Co-Creation

You are a co-creator of your life. You have a say in the direction that you're moving towards, but there are other forces that have a say as well. Everything from the celestial bodies — the Sun, the Moon, the Planets, to the microscopic world of viruses, bacteria, radiation, frequencies. All things have an influence on every other thing. Everything is in relationship to one another.

There is only a tiny sliver on the CONTROL spectrum that we actually control.

With that in mind, you are a co-creator in your Tarot readings. You set the stage by how you shuffle your cards, how you choose your cards, and deciding what spread to put them in. But the cards that you draw are face down and not consciously known. Cards drawn for a person that you have never met before and may never meet again. Another force is at work here, one you learn to trust and surrender to.

When the cards are revealed, you sort through the images in your mind, your intuition kicks in gear, and you take what you're feeling and knowing and allow a message to begin.

Let go and be in the Flow.

SUCCESS!

How do you define success? How you define it for yourself, can influence how you see it in others. You can define it by material prosperity ie. lots of money, property, or possessions. It can be defined through personal relationships with a partner, family, and community.

One can define it through their relationship with spirit, and how connected they are to a rich spiritual life. Are any of these ways of seeing success lesser or greater than another?

What do you value most in your own life? When you're able to see it in yourself, then you will recognize it in others. And help guide them towards being in their best energetic flow.

READING REVERSALS

It's good to know how a reversal can alter the energy of any given card. However, I'm not a fan of reading them. Why? Because if you open up your intuition, then you don't have to rely on the physically reversed position to indicate how you read it. Open up to feeling your way through the dynamic of the querent's situation, and take in a larger understanding of what they're going through.

As a joke, I'll tell students that instead of the meanings of 78 cards that you have to memorize, with reversals, it becomes 156. And life is too short for that. (In truth, life IS too short to memorize all those meanings.)

I'm all about learning as many layers of the Tarot that will fit within your being. But the best meanings show up while on the job. Those to me are more valid than the book meanings.

*"You're called to
add your voice
for a reason"*

Tips & Tricks

Read in as many situations as you are able ... EVERY opportunity given to you. If there are distractions around you, even better. (I once read with a crying baby next to me.)

If you always look to control your reading environment, then you can be missing out on a key ingredient of life – which is – that you don't control all the factors in your life!

There is something to be said though for a stable internet connection ...

Letting Go Is Essential

Viewing the Tarot as a "tool" is not ideal. It's about creating a partnership with the cards. A working partnership. And not one that you're looking to become a master of. Rather it is about working together and being in a state of flow.

When a magician is onstage, they're looking to control every aspect of an illusion, so that a specific outcome is reached. Not so with the Tarot. There are parts of a reading that are your responsibility, and parts that one gives to Spirit. One looks to define that relationship more and more through the experience of reading. It's not something that you can just think about. You build on that relationship by doing.

So what are some of those areas that you're responsible for? Number one, you show up in a clear mind set, show up in a state of clarity. Number two, you prepare the space for the reading. Number three, trust the process.

The Tarot may seem like a blind process. We look at the backs of the cards when they are chosen. How do we know that we're choosing the right card? The answer to that is that we don't know, not in an intellectual way. Out of all the cards in the deck, there's no way to know which of the cards will show up first. Sometimes you can have a feeling of what cards will be showing up, but let go and let the cards have their say. Read what comes up. Not what you'd like to have come up, but what is actually coming up. Trust the process.

Many times while reading, I'll think of a card and it'll come up. And that's nothing more than just being in the flow. Your place as a reader, is to be in connection with the cards. There's no forcing it. Just as the Devil card has layers of meaning about control, the more we try to force our hand, more things slip through our fingers. It's not a coincidence that the realm of Spirit is represented by water. If you hold that water tightly, the more easily it flows out of our grasp.

And so too with readings. When we're looking to control the information of what we're seeing or feeling or hearing, we can block the flow of helpful, channeled communications. Sometimes a querent is looking to control a reading. They have the outcome already set in their mind. If the cards are reflecting that, then so be it. If not, then it's your responsibility to voice otherwise. The language of spirit is not to coerce, it's not to have to be right. You give what you get, you see what you see, you give the querent the information you're receiving.

*You can
plant the seed
of an idea
within someone,
but they determine
how it will blossom.*

HUMAN BEINGS ARE A VERB

Annnnnd ... Action! We are beings in motion. Recognizing this movement is where we can invest our self towards our goals. Energy doesn't like to stand still and ***we are energy***.

Do we have a say in the type of energy we are? What type of energy would you like to infuse your actions with? With an energy of abundance, love, prosperity, determination, success?

Or with an energy of greed, limitation, fear, self-sabotage, control?

This is where our consciousness has its say. This is where we have a choice of the fuel that motivates us. What do you choose?

"Hold your cards with confidence"

MAKING FRIENDS WITH THE UNKNOWN

Does it trouble you to not know everything? One can still be confident and not know all the details of what is coming. And how is that? Know who it is that you are at your center.

If you are a kind person, then be a kind person. If you are a truth teller, then tell the truth. If you are a motivator, then do your best to motivate others. Take what it is that you know about yourself into new situations, and let them work themselves out. Are we meant for all situations. No. But by strengthening the parts of our self we're confident in, that will take us to those situations where we can be most of service.

*"Your Relationship
with Spirit
is Everything
in the Tarot"*

Commit To The Meaning

When you start pulling cards, you can start to get instant impressions or feelings, and that begins to form as a starting point in delivering your message. And it's OK to marinate in that process, to take your time.

As you start to deliver your message, it can be tempting to want to talk about all the card meanings and change your approach, especially in areas you may be uncertain about what you're feeling. And as this is not an exact science, there's no one right way to do it. You're basically creating how you operate as you go.

There are so many layers to each card of the Tarot, that when we just apply our mind to the reading, we'll look for the correct meaning. But this isn't only a process of mind, it is one of total being. Feeling, intellect, experience and values are all part of the guidance.

If we start using a scatter shot approach to reading, we'll end up watering down our words and confusing our querent. Trust that one unified message is enough to be understood. Focus on that part of your reading, instead of a desire to cover your bases and give the appearance of being right.

GIVE WHAT YOU GET

There's nothing worse than a reader who says "well, this card could mean this or it could also mean that ... and there's also a meaning of something else." This makes me crazy, and it will make your querent crazy. I understand if you're just starting out and not sure of what you're intuiting. But eventually, you'll have to stand tall in your own intuition and in your own voice, and commit to what you're seeing and hearing and feeling.

Give what you get.

Connect words to your intuition. The words that you choose are born from your relationship to Spirit, so build an area of trust between these two realms.

No reader is going to be one hundred percent accurate, but by redirecting your focus, you're looking to be of greater service. The more experience you have under your belt will give you the confidence to trust your Spirit Connection and the information you're receiving, and you will become quicker and more sure-footed with your delivery.

Give what you get.

Tips & Tricks

*Suppose you're talking to
a person about a situation,
without your Tarot cards handy.*

*Visualize a card
that comes up
in your mind's eye.*

*Draw from the
wisdom of that
particular energy.*

Uh Oh, I Just Drew One Of THOSE Cards ...

The dirty little secret with the Tarot is that all of the cards have positive and negative energy. Regardless of the image, there are layers that symbolize an easier path or where there is continued struggle.

Having said that, the groans that I hear from querents when the "heavy" cards are pulled in their reading are priceless. Death, the Devil, the Tower, almost any of the Swords, all have a visceral image that elicit a fearful reaction. And yes, the news is not always great, but more often than not, it just means that their work of moving through a difficult situation is not yet over.

We all know people who will say "Oh, that's not for me, that's for cousin Shelly's issue, what she's going through. It's not me. Pick one for me." And they go through the deck until they draw the positive card they like.

Noooo! Stop that!!

The cards that come up are the cards you get. The heavy cards help us to temper expectations. Cutting them out cheats us from having needed information to get through the difficult times.

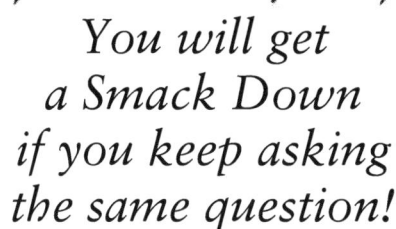

You will get a Smack Down if you keep asking the same question!

CAREER OR JOB?

Is Career and Job the same thing? I see them as very different. We can sustain ourselves with a Job, and be faithful towards it by showing up every day. But if we don't connect with the work on a soul level, then it will remain a job to do, and not a Career.

A Career is something that we were born to do. It excites us when we wake up, and fills us with a sense of meaning at day's end. We use our natural talents, acquired skills and abundant passion in having a Career, all fueled up during the course of the day. (We know it when we're not constantly looking at the clock to go home.)

In the Tarot, the Wands can point us to a soul connection for the work that we do in the world. They can indicate our passion, and show us the way to finding a career. If you've already found one, then it's about not burning ourselves out and balancing the energies to keep doing the things we love most, and finding benefit on our soul journey.

Other Career cards: The Emperor, The Eight of Pentacles, and any of the Kings.

TIPS & TRICKS

*Think of the
Knights
as cards of
Action.*

*The suit will determine
how that Knight
moves forward.*

*With determination,
playfulness, speed,
or practicality.*

*"Not everyone
will see their wings.
Not everyone
can release themselves.
Not everyone
will take off for the skies.

It's not up to you
to judge that though."*

The Reflecting Pool

One of the beautiful gifts that the Tarot can offer people is a means to see themselves. It can be a reflecting pool where they are looking at their progress or lack thereof. It becomes an ability to grow consciousness, an ability to see our strengths and weaknesses, an ability to find out who we are at our core.

The serious reader of Tarot will take it all in. Not pick and choose which flavor of the moment feels comfortable, but open to all the cards that show up, and create an honest assessment of where one is on the path.

There is always work to be done, improvements to be made, getting your act together. And if you've made progress, to acknowledge it in a way that counts. As pure gratitude, a hearty pat on the back, or an extended moment of taking it all in, storing it in your cells and your memory banks, and knowing that it's well deserved.

If you're not making progress, then keep at it. Be honest with your approach and where you're getting stuck, and look at trying some new ways.

Thank the Tarot for the insight. To be able to look at all of life in this manner is a blessing!

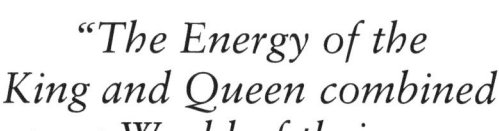

*"The Energy of the
King and Queen combined
are a World of their own.*

*The Queen sets the stage,
The King acts it out.*

There is no One without the Other.

*We all have the Masculine
and Feminine qualities.*

COMMON THREADS THAT RUN THROUGH THE CARDS

When I first started reading the Tarot, I knew about two or three different meanings for each card. I believe that's enough to start the process of reading. We initially set off reading for our self, our family, and friends. But I think that one can deepen their knowledge of the cards and open to new meanings.

Even though a lot of Tarot card decks are based on the Rider-Waite, they'll probably have some variations that we can learn from. It's on us to see if we find a resonance with that variation, if we feel equipped to be able to talk about that layer of meaning in a responsible way. Some meanings of cards can sound really great from someone else, but may not come from a place of sincerity or authenticity from us. I myself stay away from meanings that I do not resonate with.

I like to see if certain cards from other decks have similar meanings with the deck that I read from. Sometimes the cards will have a common thread of similarity, but also have layers of meaning that will take it into another direction. It can be of value to you to study these points of difference, and again to deepen your knowledge of the Tarot.

THE VAULT

How do you see yourself as a Tarot reader? Do you see yourself as a wise oracle? A sideshow fortune teller? Or maybe you see yourself as a compassionate listener and a caring friend?

If you're the gossipy type, what you can learn as a Tarot reader can fill your days and nights with a lot of material. But to be an ethical reader, one must be a keeper of secrets. One must become a vault. If you're OK with that, then your readings will be incredibly fulfilling.

How do you become a vault? Here's one thing you can do. Remember **Step One**: Everyone is a spiritual being. Know that your querent's sacred journey is not yours. You held space for them in the moment, and that was what was required. Now lock it up and let go. It's not yours to share.

TIPS & TRICKS

Pull a card.

Think of a memory that instantly comes up.

Keep Yourself Out Of The Reading

When you're reading for your querent, they want to know about themselves. Stay focused on their situation. Stay focused on helping them seeing their situation clearly. Their life may mirror our own. We may be tempted to start talking about our own life.

There will be times when reading for someone, that it will seem I'm answering a question that parallels a situation in my life. But that doesn't mean that it becomes about me. Stay focused on the querent. Examples can be powerful to illustrate a point, but when it comes to examples from our own life, it can get complicated. And what complicates it is the shift in energy, how protective we may be of our own vulnerability.

Precisely because we don't want to broadcast our weaknesses. We can shut down on having good advice if we've super-imposed our life on our querents. We can rob them of solid advice, because of how we tell our story and if we're not owning up to our own short-comings.

Stay focused on your querent and read for yourself some other time.

*"As a reader,
it's important to
'give what you get,'
to offer guidance,
but to not tell someone
what they have to do."*

WHO WANTS A HISTORY LESSON?

Now this one kind of makes me laugh, because as a younger and enthusiastic Tarot reader, I'd have a tendency to give a historical background on the cards for the querent. But for the paying customer, they weren't having any of it. People want to know what they want to know. They want to know about their situation, they want to know if they're being cheated on in a relationship or in a financial deal. They could care less about why a card means what it means. They could care less about how you as a reader, came about seeing a certain meaning unfold for the cards coming up for them.

When you go to a dentist, you're not there for them to explain how they went to dentistry school, and their trials and tribulations. You want them to apply their craft and then get out of there. The same is true for people going through a difficult situation. They want to stay focused on how they can find answers to resolve their problems, not how you got to a point of finding your way around a deck of Tarot cards.

There's a place for everything. If you want to talk about the process of becoming, then be a teacher. The classroom is a great place to share that type of information.

*"It's up to the reader to
discern where a querent is at*

*energetically, mentally,
emotionally, physically*

*and be able to craft
a meaningful message so
they can hear those words."*

*"You'll know
when it's time
to take ownership
of the title
'Tarot Reader.'*

Don't sweat it."

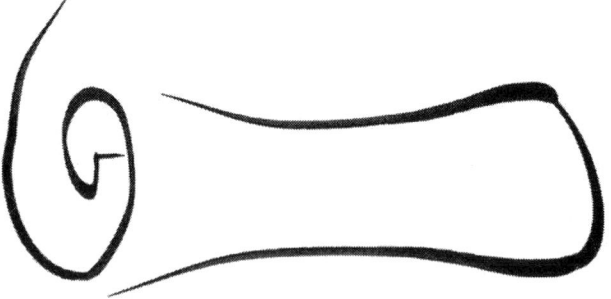

No One Is A Statue In Stone

We all have the capacity for change. In any direction, be it joy or suffering. We aren't fully set, our story is not fully written. Seeing this allows for us to create new challenges for our self and scale new heights. We can love deeper, live more fully. Find new ways of expression.

The Tarot sees everyone as a living, breathing being. That's what the cycles are all about. Yes, we can get stuck for days, months, years in a lot of different areas of life. Stuck in a job you don't like. Suffering a loss that you can't get over. But that doesn't mean it will always be like that. The Tarot helps by pointing out a direction, and you do your part in activating that direction.

OPENING UP TO NEW CARD MEANINGS

There are times when I'll pull a card, and the meanings that I'm familiar with won't apply. When that happens I recognize the opportunity for a new meaning to appear. As this'll take place in the middle of a querent reading, its where the sweating begins.

I know what's about to take place. As I'm taking in a card before me, a new layer of meaning is going to emerge from my inner consciousness. And it can take a little bit of time for new meanings to form. It's like an idea that's hatching, and so one waits for the slow cracking open of the new layer. It can start with a feeling and then slowly start to realize itself bit by bit.

Usually the new layers of meaning run pretty deep, they are not simple or shallow. I think it happens because the go-to meanings aren't sufficiently describing what the querent is going through. Along with a needed depth, another way of looking at the card is in order.

A perfect example would be the 7 of Swords. Are you the victim of thievery, or is it you taking back parts of your identity you've compromised away? Can show putting yourself back together.

Tips & Tricks

*If you're out in the world,
and looking to be
discreet in your reading,
you can always read
Playing Cards
(which came from the Tarot)
and let them guide your reading.*

*You will know
what's going down,
someone else may see
that you're just playing
a friendly card game.*

*"The Tarot is a Wheel
with many a Gear,
that spins to Cycles
in a rotating Sphere.*

We are always in motion"

Permission Granted

Are you waiting to be granted permission to be your best Spiritual self?

Well then, permission granted.

Are you needing to hear a confirmation to move forward in a direction that's calling you?

That permission is granted too.

Do you feel you live in an Abundant Universe, and have a right to explore your full potential?

Go for it! Permission is given!

Do you feel that you are worthy enough to share your voice and your experiences with others and create sacred space with them?

Absolutely you are!

Are you waiting for permission to read Tarot for yourself and others with a full heart and clear mind, an open intuition, and seeing others in their best spiritual light?

Permission granted!

"Keep It Real"

Magical Answers?

Does the Tarot give you magical answers? I think the Tarot gives you practical answers. Answers that can give you concrete steps in how you can change your life. The method to how these answers come about may seem more magical than most, but the advice can be very grounded and reasonable.

All of our situations ask that we invest ourselves in them and that we show up to do our part. The Tarot helps us see which version of our self to activate, so that our best self shines through.

Come to think of it, that does sound pretty magical.

WORDS SPECIFIC TO TAROT

Reader = The person reading the Tarot cards. They are the ones who direct a Tarot session.

Querent = The person the Reader reads Tarot for. The one with the query, or question.

Suits = Wands, Cups, Swords and Pentacles

Arcana – Arcane, Hidden

Spirit = Your spiritual source

Royalty or Court Cards = The King, Queen, Knight and Pages. One in every suit.

Other names for the Suits

Wands = Rods, Staffs, Staves, Clubs, Fire

Cups = Chalices, Goblets, Grails, Hearts, Water

Swords = Knives, Daggers, Blades, Spades, Air

Pentacles = Coins, Discs, Wheels, Diamonds, Earth

Bio

Born into a family of Psychics and Ministers, Jason D McKean, the Tarot Wizard, has read for thousands of people, and teaches Tarot online, conducts sessions in Japan, and enjoys a worldwide clientele. One of his favorite places to read Tarot is aboard the Queen Mary.

Jason's best-selling OM chant albums that include OM SANCTUARY, OM ETERNITY, and 108 SACRED OMS, are played in yoga studios and meditation halls throughout the world.

He lives in Malibu CA with his wife and dogs.

www.JasonDMcKean.com

Notes

Notes

Notes

Notes

NOTES

Notes

NOTES

Notes

Printed in Great Britain
by Amazon